THE BILLIONAIRE'S GUIDE

Unlock Wealth, Reclaim Time, Live Rich & Free

Godfred Akakpo

Enaireprenaire Books

© Godfred Akakpo @ 2025
The Billionaires Guide
1st Edition Publication Date: July, 2025
ISBN: 978-9988-52-830-0
Email:god.fredd@yahoo.com
Phone: +233 552622339

Dedication:
To those who refuse to settle for an average life. To the dreamers, the doers, and the ones who are ready to break free from the ordinary.

This book is for you,the person who is tired of trading time for money, tired of watching life pass by while stuck in a never-ending cycle. It's for the person who knows deep down that there's more to life than the daily grind. The world is full of people who wish they could change their circumstances, but this book is for the people who are ready to take action and make it happen.

To my family and mentors who have supported me with unwavering belief. Your encouragement has been the fuel to keep going.
And finally, to you, the one holding this book. May you use these words as the spark to ignite the fire within you. The path to financial, time, and mental freedom is ahead. It's your time to claim it.

"An investment in knowledge pays the best interest."

BENJAMIN FRANKLIN, THE WAY TO WEALTH (1758)

CONTENTS

FOREWORD

In today's world, true success doesn't come from working harder; it comes from working smarter.

Throughout my career, I've seen countless individuals hustle their way to financial success, but few have truly unlocked the freedom that comes with it. Most are caught in the trap of endless work, sacrificing their time, mental peace, and relationships for the illusion of success. What they don't realize is that real success is built on leverage. Leveraging your time, money, and efforts to work for you, rather than you working for them.

The Billionaire's Guide is not just a book about building wealth; it's a roadmap to true freedom, the kind of freedom that gives you the power to choose how you spend your time, where your money comes from, and how you live your life. This guide will teach you the principles of passive income, mastering your mindset, creating systems that work for you, and building the right team to support your vision.

It's time to escape the rat race. It's time to break free from the chains of traditional thinking. In these pages, you'll find practical, actionable steps that have already transformed the lives of countless individuals. Now, it's your turn.

Bishop Selasi (Vibrant Fire Ministries Int'l)

INTRODUCTION

What if everything you've been told about success, the 9-to-5 grind, the endless hustle, and the "work hard, play later" mentality was wrong?

Imagine waking up each morning with complete control over your time, your money, and your life. No more feeling chained to a job, no more sacrificing family time for a paycheck, and no more stress about money. What if your work didn't feel like work at all? What if you could build wealth while enjoying more freedom than you ever thought possible?

Welcome to The Billionaire's Guide, a transformative blueprint designed for anyone tired of the conventional path to success and ready to take control of their future. Whether you're an employee yearning for more time, a self-employed individual dreaming of more passive income, or someone simply craving real freedom, this book will show you how to make that vision a reality.

This isn't a book about "getting rich quick" or "grinding until you burn out." It's a book about working smarter, mastering your mindset, and learning how to leverage your money, time, and resources. It's about creating a life where you are no longer a slave to the clock or a paycheck, but instead have the freedom to live life on your own terms, while building wealth.

Are you ready to stop chasing success and start living it? It's time to rewrite the rules. Let's begin.

PREFACE

Thank you for picking up The Billionaire's Guide. This book was born from my own journey of starting from modest beginnings, encountering setbacks, and ultimately discovering the principles that paved the way to real financial independence.

My inspiration came from realizing how many aspiring entrepreneurs and professionals lack access to clear, practical strategies for building lasting wealth. I wrote this guide to fill that gap to share actionable insights that helped me and continue helping those striving to level up.

Within these chapters, you'll find concepts grounded in reality: mindset frameworks, financial habits, and step-by-step plans framed in plain language. Each section reflects hard-learned lessons and real-world experimentation rather than theory alone.

I also highlight how you can leverage this book as a tool: workshops, speaking events, consulting, and crowdfunding efforts. It's more than a read; it's a continual resource and roadmap.

Although short, this preface marks the starting point. Think of it as "behind the scenes" of how this book came into being. From the concept's spark to the writing process, I hope it helps you connect more deeply with the ideas and purpose driving what follows.

Welcome to The Billionaire’s Guide. Let’s get started.

Godfred Akakpo
Accra, Ghana – July 2025

PROLOGUE

At one point, I found myself staring at two diverging paths: a path marked by cautious comfort, and another paved with relentless ambition. That second path asked for everything, resilience, strategic action, and a mindset forged in clarity and purpose.

This book begins at that crossroads. Here, you're not just learning methods but you're stepping into a framework deliberately built to shape long-term wealth. Over the pages to come, you'll explore how navigating mindset, systems, and disciplined growth can transform aspiration into achievement.

Think of this prologue as a signal: what follows isn't theory. It's a toolkit crafted for people ready to think differently, act purposefully, and design their financial journey with intention.

Welcome to the start of transformation.

Godfred Akakpo

CHAPTER 1: THE RAT RACE REALITY (I)

Why You Feel Stuck -And Why You're Not Alone

"The problem is not working hard. The problem is working hard on the wrong ladder."

The Invisible Hamster Wheel

You wake up to an alarm you didn't choose, drag yourself into traffic you didn't create, and spend eight to ten hours solving problems you don't have just to get a paycheck that's spent before it hits your account.

That's the **rat race**.

It doesn't matter how well you dress it up. Nice job titles, company perks, or even a decent salary. If you're **trading time for money** without ownership, control, or freedom, you're on the wheel. And that wheel keeps spinning... faster every year.

You were never meant to survive life. You were

meant to live it. To build. To create. To experience. But the system doesn't reward that. The system rewards obedience, routine, and predictability.

Let's be clear: this is not about blaming jobs or employers. This is about asking **a deeper question**:

"Is this what I want my life to look like 10 years from now?"

For most, the answer is a quiet but painful *no*.

Meet James - A Real Story of Silent Struggle

James was 35. On paper, he had "made it." Corporate manager at a well-known tech firm. Six-figure income. Two-bedroom condo. A nice car and a packed calendar.

But James couldn't sleep. Not from stress but from **emptiness**.

Every day looked the same. Meetings. Reports. Emails. Promotions with fancier titles but heavier chains.

One night, sitting in traffic for the third hour that day, James finally whispered something most people never say out loud: "I'm not free." That moment changed everything.

He didn't quit the next day. But he started **asking different questions**. That's where true freedom begins not with money, but with a shift in mindset.

Why the Rat Race Feels Safe (But isn't)

You've been conditioned to believe that a steady job is the safest path. But here's the truth:

You can be fired in a moment.
Your income is capped.
You're taxed before you even touch your paycheck.
Your time is never truly yours.

Let's flip the script: Billionaires don't trade time for money. They build systems that do the work for them.

The real risk isn't starting something on your own. The real risk is spending your life **building someone else's dream while ignoring your own**.

The Cost of Staying on the Wheel

It's not just financial. The rat race costs you:

Time: Years pass and nothing truly changes.
Creativity: Repetition kills your ideas.
Energy: You're drained before you can work on your own goals.
Peace: Constant busyness creates background anxiety.
Potential: You forget what you're capable of.

We accept it because "everyone's doing it." But **most people are not free**, and most people are not truly wealthy.

Do you want to be "normal"? Or do you want to be free?

Birds Don't Ask for Permission to Fly

Imagine a bird in a cage with an open door. The bird doesn't leave — not because the door is locked, but because it forgot how to fly.

That's what the rat race does. It convinces you that comfort is better than freedom. That predictability is more valuable than purpose.

But you're not a bird. You're a builder, thinker, dreamer, and you don't need permission to redesign your life. What if you could:

Work less and earn more?
Build systems that pay you while you sleep?
Wake up energized instead of drained?
Own your time, your mind, and your income?

You can. That's what this book is about, showing you the mindset, tools, and systems to do exactly that.

The Wake-Up Question

Before we move on, I want you to pause. Seriously.

Take 60 seconds. Put this book down and ask yourself:

"What does freedom actually mean to me?"

Is it time with your family? Traveling without checking your bank account? Working because you want to, not because you must? Write it down. Don't skip this.

A Quick Truth Check (Belief & Truth)

"I need a stable job to survive."
You need income streams, not a job.
"I'll be free when I retire."
Why wait 30 years to live? Build freedom now.
"Starting a business is risky."
Depending on one paycheck is risky.

You Can't Escape a System You Don't Understand

That's why in the next chapter, we'll talk about mental *programming* that keeps people trapped, even after they earn more. You'll learn:

How your brain processes routine, fear, and identity
How beliefs shape your behavior (and bank account)
And how to rewire your mind for wealth and freedom

The rat race isn't just physical, it's mental. Let's break that chain next.

Chapter Challenge: The Wheel Check-In

Answer these questions in your notebook or journal:

What part of my life feels like "the wheel"?
What part of my life feels like "the sky" (freedom)?
What would my life look like if I only did what I love and what earns?
What small habit or decision could start that shift today?

Quote to Remember:

"The cage isn't locked. You're just used to it being closed."

Next Up: Chapter 2 -The Freedom of a Bird

A deeper dive into *what freedom looks like*, and how to make the leap from control to clarity.

CHAPTER 2: THE FREEDOM OF A BIRD

What It Feels Like to Finally Live on Your Own Terms

“Some birds are not meant to be caged. Their feathers are just too bright.” -Stephen King

---

You Were Born to Fly -But You Were Trained to Perch

From the moment you walk, they started teaching you how to sit.

Be quiet. Raise your hand. Color inside the lines. Follow the schedule. Stay safe. Be realistic.

It wasn’t your fault. You were born with wings and then told to never leave the ground. But deep inside, that voice never died. That voice that says:

“I’m meant for more.”
“This can’t be it.”
“I want time. Not just money.”

That's the voice of your inner bird, your **freedom instinct**. The part of you that knows life isn't meant to be lived on a schedule created by someone else.

This chapter is about remembering what freedom feels like and deciding to chase it, unapologetically.

The Bird in the Sky vs. the Bird in the Cage

Let's take a moment to imagine two birds.

Bird 1: The Caged Bird

Well-fed
Safe from predators
Lives in a gold-plated cage
Follows a schedule: wake, eat, sing, sleep
Doesn't fly, but doesn't fall either
Looks "fine" on the outside

Bird 2: The Wild Bird

Finds its own food
Faces weather, danger, and adventure
Has no predictable schedule
Soars when it wants, rests when it needs
Might fall — but always flies again
Radiates life, motion, and instinct

Which one is truly free? Now ask yourself: **Which one are you living as today?**

What Freedom Really Feels Like

Let's break this idea of "freedom" down. It's more than just quitting a job or owning a business.

Real Freedom in 3 Levels:

1. **Mental Freedom:**

No longer stressed by the opinions of others

Clear headspace, intentional choices

Confidence in your own direction

2. **Time Freedom**

Your calendar reflects *your* values

No alarms, no begging for vacation days

Time to rest, create, think, explore

3. **Financial Freedom**

You own assets, not just a job

Money flows without you chasing it

Your lifestyle isn't dependent on your next paycheck

Most people chase financial freedom first. But the billionaires? They build **mental and time freedom first** then multiply it with money.

Mini Story: A LEAP INTO THE SKY

Let me introduce you to Leah. She was a graphic designer, brilliant and creative, but buried in client emails, unpaid invoices, and 70-hour work weeks. Every dollar she made required her time. No time translates to no income.

One day, stuck between deadlines and stress migraines, she did something different. She didn't quit her job yet. But she started building a **productized service**. Templates. Courses. A YouTube channel.

Six months later, her income matched her freelance work without her doing one on one projects. A year later, she had flown from the cage.

She travels for vacation. Draws for joy again. Works 4 days a month and still makes more money than ever. She didn't escape by accident. She **built her wings** and trusted them.

How to Measure Your Current Freedom

Ask yourself these 3 freedom check-in questions:

Question

Do I control my calendar?

How long would I be okay financially if I stopped working?
Do I have energy left at the end of the day for my goals?

If your answers reveal stress, limitation, or burnout: don't panic, because it is a wakeup call.

Designing the Sky: Your Freedom Map

You can't fly without direction and here's your first practical assignment:
To create your personal **Freedom Map.**

Freedom Vision (12 months from now):
Where do you live?
What do your mornings look like?
How do you earn?
How much do you work?

Freedom Income Goal:
What's your *monthly* income goal?
How much of that will be passive or semi-passive?

Freedom Work:
What could you build, create, or automate that earnings even when you rest?

Freedom Time Goal:
What's your ideal work schedule?
How much *real free time* do you want per week?

It Starts with Permission

Most people don't feel free because they're waiting for someone to give them permission.

Permission to rest.
Permission to try something different.
Permission to be rich, creative, and happy.

You have permission to build a life of absolute freedom.

You don't need to earn it through burnout.
You don't need to wait until
you're 65.
You just need to start.

In the next chapter, we'll talk about the science behind it. How your brain holds the key to this entire journey. Once you understand how to *reprogram your mind*, everything else falls into place.

Chapter Challenge: What Would a Free Life Look Like for Me?

Take out a notebook or journal and answer:

What does a "free day" look like to me?
What am I doing now that a free person wouldn't do?
What's one way I can begin to shift toward my version of freedom this week?

Quote to Remember:

"Freedom isn't earned. It's claimed. And then built."

Next Up: Chapter 3: Rewiring the Brain for Wealth

Your brain is your most powerful financial tool. Let's start using it to create freedom, not just survive stress.

CHAPTER 3: REWIRING THE BRAIN FOR WEALTH

How to Train Your Mind to Create Money, Not Chase It

"The mind is everything. What you think, you become." - Buddha

---

You're Not Broke -You're Wired That Way

If you've ever said things like:

"I'm not good with money."
"I just need to work harder."
"Rich people got lucky..."

Then it's not just your bank account that needs a reset, it's your brain.

Most people aren't broke because they're lazy.
They're broke because they've been **conditioned to stay broke**.

Your brain has been trained to prioritize survival, not success. That's not your fault. But it *is* your responsibility to change it. Let's break it down.

How Your Brain Actually Works (in Simple Terms)

Your brain is a powerful pattern machine. It does two things really well:

1. **Seeks Familiarity**
   It craves comfort and routine even if that routine is stress, debt, or exhaustion.
2. **Protects You from Risk**
   It's wired to avoid danger but often treats new opportunities as threats.

Your thoughts become your default **filters**, and those filters become your **decisions**. Over time, those decisions shape your income, time, and identity.

The Reticular Activating System (RAS)

The RAS is a small part of your brainstem with a huge job:

It filters what you notice based on what you believe. Ever noticed how when you buy a red car, suddenly you see red cars everywhere? That's the RAS in action. It scans for what's important to you.

Now imagine if your RAS is constantly scanning

for:

"Money is hard to get"

"I'm not lucky"
"I don't deserve more"

That's what your brain starts to find and a **proof that wealth isn't for you.**

But here's the good news: you can *train your RAS* to scan for abundance, opportunities, leverage, and wealth and that starts with your thoughts.

From Scarcity Thinking to Billionaire Thinking Let's compare two mindsets:

Scarcity Mindset
"I need to work more hours."
"I can't afford it."
"I'll never be like them."

Billionaire Mindset
"How can I get results with less effort?"
"How can I afford it creatively?"
"Money flows through systems I create."
"What habits, beliefs, and actions got them there?"

You can literally *rewire your brain* to think like a billionaire by changing:

The language you use daily
The questions you ask yourself

The beliefs you reinforce

Mini Story: From Fear to Fortune
Marcus was raised to believe that money was evil. Growing up, every argument in his house was about bills, debt, or what they couldn't afford.

Even when he started making good money in his mid-30s, he always lost it. Bad investments, failed businesses, even self-sabotage.

It wasn't until he started working with a mentor who showed him his beliefs were the problem, not his business plan and then things changed.

Marcus began journaling, visualizing success, and surrounding himself with wealth-minded people. Three years later, he was earning 10x more but more importantly, he felt **free**.

---

5 Mental Habits That Create Wealth

Here are five ways to start retraining your brain right now:

Repetition of Wealth Thoughts
Say your affirmations daily.
Example: "I am a creator of wealth through systems."

Visual Triggers
Use vision boards, phone wallpapers, or make notes with goals and power words.

Journaling with Intention
Write your desired future like it's already real:
"I work 4 hours a day and earn $20k/month."

Gratitude for What's Coming
Feel grateful in advance. Gratitude aligns your emotions with abundance.

Audit Your Inputs
Cut out negativity, scarcity-driven news, or broke-thinking people.
The brain becomes what you feed it mentally, emotionally, and spiritually.

Train Your Brain with This 5-Minute

Daily Practice Here's a quick morning ritual

to rewire your mindset daily:

1. **Affirmation:** "I create systems that earn money while I sleep."
2. **Visualization:** Picture your freedom lifestyle vividly where are you, what are you doing?
3. **Gratitude:** Write down 3 things you're grateful for now and future based.
4. **Declaration:** Say out loud, "I decide who I become, and I become wealthy."
5. **Silence or Meditation:** Just 1 or 2 minutes of

silence to anchor the shift.

What Happens When You Rewire Your Mind?

You stop chasing and start **attracting**.
You stop hoarding and start **multiplying**.
You stop surviving and start **strategizing**.

This is how billionaires think, not with panic, but with **pattern recognition** and **mental clarity**.

They've built their freedom first in their mind and then turned it into reality.

Chapter Challenge: Brain Reset Blueprint

In your notebook or journal, answer:

1. What are the 3 money beliefs I picked up growing up?
2. Are they helping me or holding me back?
3. Write 1 new money belief you choose to install today.
4. What can I do this week to reinforce that belief?

Quote to Remember:
"Your brain is a garden. What you plant becomes your life."

Next Up: Chapter 4 - The Power of Decision

It's not your conditions; it's your decision to shape

your future. Learn how to decide like a billionaire and act with clarity, speed, and confidence.

CHAPTER 4: THE POWER OF DECISION

The One Habit That Separates Billionaires from Everyone Else

"Indecision is the thief of opportunity." - Jim Rohn

Decide, or Be Decided For

Every day, life is asking you questions:

Will you stay or leave?
Will you build or react?
Will you choose growth or comfort?

And if you don't decide... the world will decide for you.

Your job will decide how much your time is worth. Your bills will decide how much freedom you have. Your fears will decide what you never try.

Most people aren't stuck because they lack talent.

They're stuck because they've never truly decided to be free.

Billionaires Decide Fast and Correct Later

Here's something you'll notice about high-level entrepreneurs and investors:
They make **fast, clear decisions** even with limited information.

Then, they make micro adjustments quickly if needed.

This is known as **decide → commit → correct**.

Meanwhile, most people wait for perfect clarity and get paralyzed by overthinking.

Here's what billionaires know:

Speed = momentum

Clarity comes from action, not more thinking

You can't steer a parked car

Story: The $100K Decision That Took 10 Minutes

A mentor of mine once sat in a room with a well-known digital entrepreneur. She was presented with an opportunity to acquire a small online platform for $100K.
Within 10 minutes, she said yes. Not because she was reckless.
Because she had already built **decision filters**.

She knew her numbers.
She knew her growth strategy.
She knew the difference between fear and facts.

The average person might take weeks by then; the deal would be gone.

The Decision Delay Trap

Let's break this down:

Hesitation is a decision.
(You're saying "no" by not saying "yes.")

Overthinking is a symptom of fear.
(Usually fear of judgment, failure, or risk.)

Too many options = paralysis.
(Freedom doesn't come from more choices but it comes from aligned ones.)

Here's what you need: **a decision framework.**

The 3-Step Billionaire Decision Method

Use this filter every time you feel stuck:

1. **Clarity: What really matters here?**
    - What is the *outcome* I want?
    - What are the *non-negotiables*?
    - What would future-me thank me for?
2. **Courage: Am I avoiding or aligning?**
    - Is this decision aligned with my vision, or my

fear?

- What's the **worst** that could happen?
- Will I regret *not* trying?

3. **Correction: How can I course-correct fast?**

- Can I test this decision quickly?
- What's the *minimum viable action* I can take now?
- What's my backup plan if it flops?

Make the decision. Then make the decision *right* by following through.

Billionaire Filter: The YES/NO Matrix

Use this tool to cut through noise and get clear, fast:

Question (If YES → Move Forward, IF No- Eliminate)

Does this move me closer to

my freedom goal?

Does it align with my

values and vision?

Does it multiply my income or time?

Does it give me leverage,

not just work?

If it's not a **HELL YES**, it's a **NO**.

Avoiding Decision Fatigue

Every decision you make burns brain energy.

That's why billionaires **simplify** the small stuff (clothes, meals, routines) so they have mental space for big decisions.

You can do the same:

- Set default meals, morning routines, and habits.
- Create a daily decision checklist.
- Batch small choices (e.g. content planning, errands, money reviews).

Fewer small decisions = better big ones.

Mini Practice: Decision Journaling

Start writing these prompts daily:

- What decisions did I avoid today?
- What decision do I need to make even if I'm afraid?
- What's the smallest next action I can take?

Clarity isn't always found, it's **built**.

Chapter Challenge: Decide Something Today

Pick one thing you've been putting off and:

1. Apply the 3-Step Decision Method.
2. Write your answer down.

3. Take the first micro-action before the end of the day.

Remember: momentum builds faster when you move.

Quote to Remember:

"Successful people make decisions quickly and change them slowly.
Unsuccessful people do the opposite."
- Napoleon Hill

Next Up: Chapter 5 -The Law of Attraction (With Action)

Now that you've decided, we're going to align your inner focus with outer results the right way. Manifestation meets systems.

CHAPTER 5: THE LAW OF ATTRACTION (WITH ACTION) (I)

How to Manifest Wealth Without Sitting in a Dark Room Humming

---

"You don't attract what you want. You attract what you are." - Dr. Joe Dispenza

---

The Problem with "Manifestation Culture"

Let's be real: the law of attraction has been both **revolutionary** and **misunderstood**.

A lot of people think:

- "If I just think about money, it will come."
- "If I vibe high enough, the universe will pay me."
- "If I wait long enough, my dreams will appear."

But here's the truth:

The universe doesn't respond to dreams. It responds to decisions.

Manifestation is **real** but it's not magic. It's *mental alignment + focused action*.

So, What *Is* the Law of Attraction?

At its core, the law of attraction says:

"What you consistently focus on, you move toward."

Your thoughts shape your emotions.
Your emotions shape your energy.
Your energy influences your
behavior. Your behavior
builds your results.

If you focus daily on:

- **Scarcity** → You'll act in fear and play small.
- **Abundance** → You'll act in confidence and attract opportunity.

This isn't just spiritual, it's neurological.

Your brain literally **filters** and **amplifies** the energy you focus on.

Where Most People Get It Wrong

1. **They visualize without action.**
(They dream, but don't move.)

2. **They take action without vision.** (They hustle, but don't know what they want.)
3. **They try to manifest from fear.** ("I hope this fixes my life" = desperate energy.)

Billionaires use the law of attraction but with intentional focus, strategic planning, and ruthless execution.

Story: How a Vision Became Reality in 18 Months

Dalia worked in a bank. Every day felt like quiet suffocation.
One day, she created a **vision board** not just with cars and cash, but with her ideal day:

- Morning yoga in Bali
- $15K/month from online products
- Clients she loved working with
- Writing a book and speaking on stages

Every morning for the next year, she looked at that board and asked:

"What's the next small action I can take to move toward this life?"

She launched a simple course. Then built a YouTube channel.
Then took her first client.
Then automated 80% of her income.

She didn't wait for the universe to bless her.
She **aligned her actions with her intentions**.

Today, she lives that exact life.

The Formula: Attraction = Alignment
Here's a practical model to follow:

VISION → EMOTION → BELIEF → ACTION → RESULT

VISION: Get clear on what you want
EMOTION: Feel it like it's real
BELIEF: Reinforce that it's possible
ACTION: Take bold, consistent steps

RESULT: Receive the outcome (and repeat) If one

link is missing the chain breaks.

Build Your Wealth Attraction Routine

Here's how you train your brain to attract what you want:

1. Create a Vision Board

- Include: income goals, lifestyle, experiences, environment
- Use real photos, not just Pinterest glam
- Put it somewhere you'll see daily

2. Script Your Future Life

- Every morning or night, write a paragraph: *"I*

wake up energized in my beach home. I check my Stripe account and $1,200 came in overnight..."

3. Feel the Emotion First

- The brain can't tell the difference between real and vividly imagined.
- Feel gratitude **before** it arrives. Gratitude is the signal of "already having."

4. Take Inspired Action

- Ask yourself: "What would the wealthy version of me do today?" • Then do it even if it's scary or small.

Aligning with the Law of Action

Faith without works is dead. So is manifestation without movement.

Here's how the universe works:

-You say "I want freedom"
-You visualize and believe
-Then you get tested:

a. A new opportunity shows up

b. A risk appears
c. A challenge stretches your courage

Most people reject it and say, "It didn't work." But that *was* the work.

Your *reaction* to opportunity is your application of faith.

Chapter Challenge: Build a Mini Vision Board

You can do this digitally (Canva, Pinterest) or physically.

Include:

- A screenshot of your ideal income
- A calendar with 3 work days/week
- A photo of your dream workspace
- A quote that moves you
- One picture that represents absolute freedom to you

Look at it for 3 minutes every day. Then ask:

"What can I do *today* that moves me closer to this?"

Quote to Remember:

"The universe doesn't give you what you want. It gives you what you're willing to become."

Next Up: Chapter 6 - Cashflow is King

Ready to turn energy into earnings? We're about to dive into how billionaires manage, multiply, and master their money starting with cashflow.

CHAPTER 6: CASHFLOW IS KING

How to Manage, Multiply, and Master Your Money Like a Billionaire

---

"Wealth consists not in having great possessions, but in having few wants." - Epictetus

---

The True Power of Cashflow

If you want to be financially free, **cashflow** is your best friend.
Wealthy people don't just chase big paychecks. They create *streams* of money that flow consistently, regardless of their active work.

Active income is the money you earn by working for someone or trading your time for money.
Passive income is money that comes to you whether you work or not through investments, systems, and intellectual property.

But here's the catch:

Cashflow is the bridge that connects **active income** to **passive income**.

You want your cashflow to be *systematic*. To make money while you sleep, you must design processes that continuously bring in income, no matter where you are or what you're doing.

The Billionaire's Approach to Cashflow

Let's break down how billionaires think about cashflow:

1. **Investing for Recurring Income**
   Billionaires don't just buy things. They buy **assets** that provide *continuous returns*. Real estate properties that generate rental income. Dividend-paying stocks. Business ventures that run themselves with smart teams and systems
2. **Building Systems for Income**
   Instead of relying on hourly work, wealthy individuals build systems.
   They build businesses that make money while they sleep. **Systems** are repeatable, scalable, and can run themselves with the right automation and outsourcing.

3. **Leverage & Outsourcing**

Wealthy people know they don't need to do everything. They leverage time, skills, and money from others to build cashflow.

You can do the same by: Hiring a team, partnering with people who complement your skills, Automating your business processes

4. **Focus on Cashflow - Not Just the Total Wealth**
Billionaires know the importance of regular, predictable cashflow. It's not about having $100M net worth; it's about **how much cash you can consistently produce**.
They often structure their investments and businesses to generate cashflow first, wealth later.

The Cashflow Quadrant

There's a concept popularized by Robert Kiyosaki- the Cashflow Quadrant, which breaks down four types of income earners:

Quadrant

E (Employee): Works for someone else. For example, corporate jobs, service, trading time for money industry.

S (Self-employed) : Works for themselves. For example, Freelancers, small business trading time for money

B (Business Owners): Owns a business that works.

For example, Entrepreneurs, franchise Owner)

I (Investor): Makes money through Real estate, stocks, bonds, investments and assets and venture capitalists .

To build true wealth and time freedom, you want to move from **E** and **S** (where you are trading time for money) to **B** and **I** (where money works for you).

Story: From Freelancer to Cashflow King

Lena was a successful freelance designer. She earned a decent income, but the cycle of working for clients, meeting deadlines, and constantly hustling left her drained.
After a conversation with a mentor, Lena shifted her focus:

- She started creating digital products like design templates, which she could sell passively.
- She invested in rental properties that produced monthly cashflow.
- She hired other designers to manage client projects.

Today, Lena makes more money in a month than she did in a year as a freelancer. She learned to **multiply** her time by leveraging **systems** and **assets**.

The Millionaire Cashflow Formula:

Here's a simple formula for **building** and **managing** your own cashflow:

1. **Start with Active Income**
   Get a steady, reliable income stream that can be saved and reinvested. If you're already in a job or business, use this as your foundation.
2. **Automate Savings**
   Create a system to save a portion of your income automatically
   (20% is a good start). Don't wait for "extra" money. Pay yourself first.
3. **Invest for Passive Income**
   Buy assets that generate income (real estate, dividend stocks, businesses). Choose investments that provide consistent returns, rather than hoping for big wins.
4. **Build Scalable Systems**
   Invest in systems (businesses, processes) that can work without your constant involvement. The goal is to create an asset that generates consistent cashflow whether you're working or not.
5. **Reinvest and Diversify**

   Reinvest profits into new income streams. Diversify your portfolio to protect against risk and grow your wealth faster.

Action Steps for Building Cashflow

-Track Your Current Cashflow

Create a budget. What are you spending, and what are you earning? Identify your active income and where you can save.

-Invest in Your First Passive Income Stream

Start small. Invest in something with a low barrier to entry (stocks,real estate crowdfunding, peer-to-peer lending).

-Automate What You Can

Set up automatic savings, bill payments, and even incomegenerating systems (like selling digital products or using affiliate marketing).

-Work on Building a Scalable Business

Create a system that can work without your direct involvement. Look into e-commerce, digital products, or online services that can scale.

-Reinvest Your Profits

When you earn passive income, use it to buy more assets or invest in cashflow-generating projects. This turns your earnings into **exponential growth**.

Chapter Challenge: Build Your Cashflow Plan

Take 10 minutes to answer the following:

1. What's my current monthly cashflow from my active income?
2. What's one passive income stream I can start

today?

3. How can I automate savings or reinvest profits to increase my cashflow?
4. What's a business or system I could start to create income that doesn't depend on my time?

Quote to Remember:

"You're not truly wealthy until your money works for you."
- Tony Robbins

Next Up: Chapter 7 -The Freedom of a Bird

It's not just about financial freedom, it's about total *life* freedom. Let's explore the lifestyle, the mindset, and the choices that create true independence.

CHAPTER 7: THE FREEDOM OF A BIRD

How to Live a Life of True Freedom Beyond Money

"The freedom of the bird comes not from flying aimlessly, but from knowing where it is going."
- Unknown

True Freedom: More Than Just Money

When most people dream of freedom, they think of:

- **Financial freedom** -the ability to stop trading time for money.
- **Time freedom** -the ability to choose how to spend your day.
- **Mental freedom**-the ability to live without stress, anxiety, or limitations.

But what if I told you that freedom isn't just a financial goal? True freedom is a

lifestyle. It's about building a life where you don't just escape the rat race but you **design** your life, based on your deepest values and desires. This is what billionaires do. They build businesses, systems, and structures that allow them to live life on their terms.

The goal isn't just to escape your current job or routine; it's about **creating a life that fits your vision** of freedom.

The Three Pillars of Freedom

1. **Mental Freedom**

- Mental freedom is about letting go of limiting

beliefs and patterns.

- It's about rewiring your brain to think and feel like the version of yourself who's already wealthy and free.
- Mental freedom allows you to take risks, face challenges, and move through fear without getting paralyzed.

2. Time Freedom

- Time freedom is the ability to choose how you spend your day, without being forced into a specific routine.
- It's flexibility to work when you want, take vacations when you need, and spend time with

people who matter most.

- Time freedom gives you the ability to say "no" to things that drain you, and "yes" to things that nourish your soul.

3. Financial Freedom

- Financial freedom is the result of managing money, building assets, and leveraging systems so that money works for you, not the other way around.
- It's having **enough passive income** to cover your living expenses, allowing you to focus on building more freedom, rather than just working for survival.

Story: The Freedom of a Bird

A billionaire entrepreneur named Simon spent the first 20 years of his career grinding through the corporate world. He had the high-paying job, the title, the connections but he was burned out. He had no time for himself, no time for family, and his mental health was deteriorating.

One day, he asked himself:

- "What would my life look like if money wasn't an issue?"
- "What if I didn't need to work to survive?"

That day, Simon sold off some of his companies and restructured his investments to focus on building passive income streams. Over time, he freed himself from the 9-to-5 grind and started living a life aligned with his values:

- He built a foundation for young entrepreneurs.
- He traveled the world with his family.
- He created art and started learning new skills.

Simon wasn't just wealthy; he had **freedom** in every sense of the word. His passive income allowed him to pursue his passions, take his time back, and live life on his terms.

The Real Freedom Formula

If you want to experience true freedom, follow this simple framework:

1. Clarify Your Values

What does freedom *really* mean to you? Is it:
More time with your family? The ability to travel at will? The chance to work on meaningful projects?

Understanding what matters most helps you align your life and wealth with your **true desires**. This clarity is essential.

2. Design Your Life

Once you know your values, design your lifestyle. What kind of work can you do that gives you both freedom and fulfillment?
How can you balance work, play, and rest?

Build a schedule that serves you, not the other way around. The **wealthy** know that time is their most precious resource.

3. Create Systems of Leverage

Leverage is how you gain freedom. Instead of trading time for money, find ways to create recurring revenue or build assets that generate wealth without you having to constantly show up.

4. Remove Mental Barriers

Mental freedom comes from letting go of fear, judgment, and self-doubt. It's about retraining your mind to think **abundantly**. Wealthy individuals live by the mindset that *anything is possible,* and they focus on creating solutions instead of dwelling on problems.

How to Achieve Time Freedom: A Practical Approach

Time freedom doesn't come from doing less — it comes from being intentional about **how** and **when** you work. Here's how to design a life with maximum freedom:

1. Outsource & Automate

- Start delegating tasks that take up your time, but don't align with your highest value work.
- Use automation tools (like scheduling apps, email responders, and business systems) to minimize the time you spend on repetitive

tasks.

2. Create a Freedom Schedule

- Plan your week in a way that protects your time for personal growth, family, and passion projects.
- Schedule work around your personal life, not the other way around.

3. Invest in Leverage

- Invest in income-generating assets, like real estate or stocks, that make money for you while you focus on other activities.
- Build businesses that run with minimal involvement.

The Freedom Mindset: Abundance vs. Scarcity

To live a life of freedom, you must embrace an abundance mindset not just in money, but in all areas of life. This is the foundation of every billionaire's philosophy:

- **Scarcity Mindset**: Believes there's never enough money, more time, more opportunities. It leads to fear driven decisions.
- **Abundance Mindset**: Knows there's more than enough for everyone, and the key to success is in collaboration, innovation, and value creation. An abundance mindset isn't just a spiritual concept, it's **practical**. It allows you to take risks, collaborate, and create opportunities

that others miss because they are too focused on scarcity and competition.

Mini Practice: Create Your Freedom Vision

Take a few minutes today to answer these questions:

- If money and time were no longer issues, what would your ideal day look like?
- What would you do with your time if you had true freedom?
- What values are most important to you when designing your life?

Quote to Remember:

"The greatest wealth is to live content with little." - Plato

---

Next Up: Chapter 8 -The Habits of Highly Effective People

We're diving into the daily routines and habits that create long-term success and personal freedom.

CHAPTER 8: THE HABITS OF HIGHLY EFFECTIVE PEOPLE

How to Cultivate the Daily Routines That Lead to Lasting Success

---

"Success is the sum of small efforts, repeated day in and day out." -Robert Collier

---

The Power of Habits in Building Wealth

When we look at billionaires and successful people, it's easy to think they were just born with special gifts or that they were lucky. But much of their success is built on the foundation of **effective habits**. In fact, successful people don't just work harder, they work **smarter** and **more consistently**. Their daily habits set them up for success in ways that compound over time.

It's these small, intentional actions that add up, turning ordinary days into extraordinary years. Whether you're focused on building your career, growing a business, or making passive income, the habits you adopt will determine how quickly you get to your goals.

The 7 Key Habits of Highly Effective People

Here's a breakdown of the habits that billionaires and high achievers consistently practice:

1. Start with Clarity (Purpose and Vision)

- **Highly effective people** wake up every day with clarity. They know their "why" and have a clear vision for where they want to go.
- They write down their goals and update them regularly.
- Your habits should start with a vision of what you want to achieve. This clarity provides motivation and direction.

2. Daily Planning and Prioritization

Highly effective people plan their day the night before. They set their priorities, ensuring that they focus on **high-impact tasks** that bring them closer to their goals.
Stephen Covey, author of *The 7 Habits of Highly Effective People*, suggests focusing on **important** but **not urgent** tasks, which helps you avoid

spending time on distractions.

3. Consistency Over Perfection

- Successful people embrace consistency. They know that **progress, not perfection**, is key.
- Whether it's fitness, reading, learning, or creating wealth, consistency wins. It's the habit of showing up every day, even when motivation fades.

4. Time Blocking and Focused Work

- Time blocking is a technique used by many high achievers. It's about dedicating specific chunks of your day to focused, uninterrupted work.
- Use a **Pomodoro technique** or time blocks of 45-60 minutes of focused work, followed by short breaks. This minimizes distractions and maximizes productivity.

5. Continuous Learning and Growth

- The most successful people never stop learning. They read books, attend seminars, listen to podcasts, and invest in personal development.
- Bill Gates reads 50 books a year. Warren Buffett spends five to six hours a day reading. Knowledge is power, but **applied knowledge** is wealth.

6. Healthy Body, Healthy Mind

- Wealth and success are not just about money

— they're about your overall well-being.

- Successful people prioritize health through daily exercise, proper nutrition, and rest. They know that mental and physical energy are the keys to sustained productivity.
- Exercise isn't just about physical health; it also sharpens mental clarity, focus, and creativity.

7. Gratitude and Reflection

- Effective people start their day by reflecting on what they're grateful for. They practice daily gratitude, which helps them stay grounded and positive.

  They also take time to reflect on their actions at the end of each day, tweaking their approach and learning from mistakes.
- Reflecting on your progress keeps you on track and helps you learn from setbacks.

Story: How Consistency Built a Million-Dollar Brand

Angela started her e-commerce business while working full-time at a corporate job. At first, she worked on her business just a few hours a week. But she committed to being **consistent** and that changed everything.

Here's what she did:

- **Planning**: Every Sunday, Angela would map out her goals for the week and time-block 5-10 hours to work on her business. She treated these hours as non-negotiable.

- **Focus**: She would focus only on tasks that directly impacted her business no distractions. Email, social media, and other distractions were kept out of her work blocks.
- **Learning**: Angela spent 30 minutes every day reading books and listening to podcasts about marketing, entrepreneurship, and branding.
- **Growth**: By the end of the year, her businesses exploded. She went from making $200/month to over $10K/month.
- **Mindset**: Even when things got tough, she maintained gratitude and stayed positive. She celebrated her small wins and used setbacks as learning experiences.

After two years, Angela was able to quit her corporate job and focus on her business full-time. Her consistent habits paid off.

Building Your Daily Success Habits

To build your own set of habits, here's a practical guide to follow:

1. Write Down Your Goals and Habits

- Be specific about what you want to achieve and the habits that will get you there. Don't just think about them then **write them down** and review them regularly.

2. Time-Block Your Day

Set specific hours for work, exercise, learning, and leisure. Don't leave your schedule to chance. Having a structured day will help you stay productive and focused.

3. Start Small, Then Build Up

- Begin with **one habit** at a time. Don't overwhelm yourself by trying to change everything at once.
- For example, start with reading 15 minutes a day, then increase it to 30 minutes as it becomes a part of your routine.
- Once you've mastered one habit, add another.

4. Track Your Progress

- Track your daily habits to ensure consistency. Use habit tracking apps or a simple journal to mark your progress.
- This helps you stay accountable and motivated.

5. Accountability and Mentorship

- Find a mentor or accountability partner. Check in regularly to share your progress, setbacks, and wins.
- Accountability partners are powerful because they hold you to your commitments.

6. Celebrate Small Wins

- Don't wait until you hit a big goal to celebrate.

Celebrate the small, everyday wins. This will keep you motivated and reinforce positive behavior.

Mini Practice: Create Your Own Success Routine

1. **List 3 Key Habits** you want to develop that will bring you closer to your financial or personal freedom goals.
2. **Time-block** your daily schedule and allocate time to work on these habits every day.
3. **Track your progress** and reflect on how these habits are moving you toward your vision.

Quote to Remember:

"Successful people are simply those with successful habits." -Brian Tracy

---

Next Up: Chapter 9 - The Rat Race

Now that you've learned about the habits that lead to success, it's time to break free from the **rat race** and take control of your life. In this chapter, we'll discuss how to stop living paycheck to paycheck and make choices that align with your goal

CHAPTER 9: THE RAT RACE (II)

How to Break Free from the Cycle and Build a Life of Freedom

"The problem with the rat race is that even if you win, you're still a rat." - Lily Tomlin

---

The Rat Race: An Endless Cycle

We've all heard the term "rat race". That cycle where you wake up, go to work, collect your paycheck, pay your bills, rinse and repeat. It's the everyday struggle where you feel like you're stuck in a loop, chasing money but never quite feeling free.

The rat race is:

- Working long hours for someone else's benefit.
- Living paycheck to paycheck, with no room for savings or investment.

- Constantly worrying about how to pay your bills and handle your financial responsibilities.
- Feeling stuck because you depend on your job to survive, and don't know how to break the cycle.

Many people don't even realize they're in the rat race. They've been conditioned to accept that this is how life works. Work hard, get paid, pay your bills, and hope for the best. But this cycle isn't necessary, and it's possible to break free if you change your approach to money, time, and life.

Why the Rat Race Keeps People Trapped

1. Fear and Scarcity Mentality

Many people stay in the rat race because they fear losing their job or financial security. o "What if I can't find another job?" o "What if I fail in my business?"

This fear keeps them playing it safe, never daring to think beyond the current situation. This scarcity mindset focuses on limitations rather than opportunities.

2. Lack of Financial Education

The traditional education system doesn't teach financial independence or how to manage money. People often grow up without understanding how to make their money work for them. They work hard but don't know how to build wealth.

3. **Living Beyond Your Means**
   In today's consumer-driven world, it's easy to overspend. People buy things they don't need with money they don't have to impress others. This lifestyle leads to constant debt and financial pressure, keeping them chained to their job.

4. **Staying in Comfort Zones**
   The rat race is comfortable in a way. It's predictable, and the fear of stepping out of that comfort zone often keeps people stuck. The idea of **risk** and the unknown stops people from making the leap to financial independence and personal freedom.

Breaking Free: The Key to Escaping the Rat Race

The first step to breaking free from the rat race is realizing that **you are not stuck**. You could take control of your life, build wealth, and design a life that gives you freedom, both financial and personal. Here's how you can escape the cycle:

1. Mindset Shift: From Employee to Entrepreneur

Billionaires and successful people don't think like employees but they think like entrepreneurs.

- **Employees** trade their time for money.
- **Entrepreneurs** create value and build systems that generate passive income.

You don't have to quit your job to think like an entrepreneur. Start small by focusing on developing **additional streams of income**, like:

- Freelancing or consulting
- Creating and selling digital products
- Investing in real estate or stocks
- Starting a side business or passion project

Shifting your mindset will help you start thinking about **creating** rather than just working.

2. Living Below Your Means

To escape the rat race, you need to build **financial discipline**. This means learning to live below your means.

- Create a budget, and prioritize saving and investing.
- Focus on assets that generate income, rather than liabilities that drain your wealth.
- It's not about depriving yourself, but about making intentional choices with your money.

By keeping your expenses low and investing wisely, you can create a cushion that allows you to take more risks and make choices that move you toward freedom.

3. Build Passive Income

The key to breaking free from the rat race is **passive income**. Passive income allows you to earn money without constantly working for it. Here are a few ways to start building passive income streams:

- **Real Estate**: Owning rental properties that provide consistent cashflow.
- **Investments**: Dividend-paying stocks or bonds.
- **Digital Products**: Creating content, courses, or eBooks that generate ongoing revenue.
- **Online Business**: Setting up automated businesses that require minimal daily involvement.

The more passive income you can generate, the less you rely on your job to survive.

4. Develop Financial Education

You must educate yourself about money. Financial literacy is one of the most important factors in breaking free from the rat race. Start by reading books, listening to podcasts, and taking courses on:

- Money management
- Investing
- Business and entrepreneurship

The more you understand how money works, the easier it will be to take control of your finances and begin building wealth.

5. Create an Exit Plan

An exit plan is your strategy for leaving the rat race. It's not about quitting your job tomorrow. It's about having a clear roadmap for financial independence. Here's how to create an exit plan:

- **Set clear financial goals**: Define how much money you need to live off passive income and create a timeline.
- **Start building assets**: Focus on investments and income-generating projects that will provide you with enough passive income to replace your active income.
- **Track your progress**: Regularly assess how close you are to your goal and adjust your strategies as needed.

Story: The Man Who Escaped the Rat Race

David worked at a corporate job for over 15 years. He was constantly climbing the ladder, working overtime, and living paycheck to paycheck. Despite earning a high salary, he never felt truly free.

One day, after attending a seminar on financial independence, David realized he was stuck in the rat race. He knew he needed to make a change.

Here's what he did:

- **Mindset Shift**: He stopped thinking like an employee and started learning about investments and creating passive income streams.
- **Living Below His Means**: David cut down on unnecessary expenses and started saving

aggressively.

- **Building Passive Income**: He bought rental properties, invested in dividend stocks, and started a small online business.
- **Financial Education**: He spent time each week learning about money and how to make it work for him.

Within 5 years, David had enough passive income to cover his living expenses. He quit his corporate job, started traveling, and worked on projects that truly excited him.

Action Steps to Escape the Rat Race

1. **Shift Your Mindset**: Start thinking like an entrepreneur. What skills can you monetize? What side hustle can you start today?
2. **Live Below Your Means**: Track your expenses and start saving aggressively. Cut out unnecessary spending.
3. **Start Building Passive Income**: Invest in real estate, stocks, or create a side business that generates income while you sleep.
4. **Educate Yourself About Money**: Commit to learning about finance, investing, and wealth-building strategies.
5. **Create Your Exit Plan**: Set a clear financial goal and roadmap for leaving the rat race and achieving financial independence.

Quote to Remember:

"The rat race is a system designed to keep you from escaping. It's up to you to break free."
-Unknown

Next Up: Chapter 10 - The Vision Board

We've covered financial freedom strategies. Now, let's focus on creating a clear vision of your ideal life. In this chapter, we'll dive into the power of vision boards to manifest your dreams and goals.

CHAPTER 11: THE LAW OF ATTRACTION (II)

How to Attract the Life You Want by Aligning Your Thoughts and Actions

---

"Ask for what you want and be prepared to get it."
-Maya Angelou

Understanding the Law of Attraction

The Law of Attraction is a powerful and universal principle that states: **like attracts like**. In simple terms, what you focus on your thoughts, feelings, and beliefs shapes your reality. The energy you emit is attracted back to you in the form of people, opportunities, and circumstances.

This law is at work in your life, whether you consciously understand it or not. The key to using it to your advantage is learning how to align your thoughts and actions with the outcomes you want to manifest.

The Law of Attraction is based on the idea that everything in the universe is energy. Your thoughts are energy, and they have the ability to **attract** or **repel** different experiences into your life. If you focus on positive thoughts, abundance, and success, you'll attract positive opportunities. If you focus on fear, negativity, or scarcity, you'll attract more of those things as well.

The Science Behind the Law of Attraction

While the Law of Attraction is often discussed in spiritual and philosophical terms, there's actually a scientific basis for it. Neuroscience, quantum physics, and psychology all provide evidence that our thoughts can influence our reality:

1. Neuroplasticity

The human brain is capable of forming new neural pathways, meaning our thoughts can literally reshape our brains. When you focus on positive, abundant thoughts, you create new, empowering pathways that influence your behaviors and experiences.

2. The Reticular Activating System (RAS)

The RAS is a part of your brain that filters information and brings your attention to things that align with your current focus or belief systems. When you think about your goals, the RAS helps you recognize opportunities related to those goals. For example, if you focus on abundance, you'll start noticing wealth-building opportunities you would have previously overlooked.

3. Quantum Physics

Quantum physics tells us that energy and matter are connected, and that at the subatomic level, particles behave according to the observer's expectations. This concept aligns with the Law of Attraction: when you focus on a specific goal or desire, you're sending out a vibrational frequency that attracts corresponding energy from the universe.

The Three Main Principles of the Law of Attraction

There are three essential steps to successfully

using the Law of Attraction:

1. Ask

The first step in attracting what you want is to **clearly define** your desires. Ask for what you want, whether it's financial freedom, success in your business, better health, or meaningful relationships.

Be specific and clear in your requests. Instead of simply thinking, "I want to be rich," say, "I want to earn $100,000 in passive income by the end of the year." The more specific you are, the more clearly the universe can align opportunities to match your desires.

2. Believe

Once you've asked, the next step is to **believe** that what you want is already on its way. Belief is essential because doubt and fear act as blocks to manifestation. To manifest your desires, you must believe that you are deserving of them and that they are already becoming a part of your reality.

Affirmations, visualization, and meditation are powerful tools for reinforcing belief. When you see yourself already achieving your goal, your belief strengthens, and you become more open to receiving what you desire.

3. Receive

The final step is to **receive** what you've asked for. Receiving requires you to be open and ready to accept abundance in all forms. You must be willing to take action, remain receptive, and trust that the universe is guiding you toward your goals.

Remember, the Law of Attraction isn't just about wishful thinking. You have to align your actions with your desires. This means setting clear goals, making consistent progress, and staying open to the unexpected ways in which opportunities may show up.

How to Use the Law of Attraction in Your Life

Here are some practical ways you can begin using the Law of Attraction to manifest your desires:

1. Create a Clear Vision

Take the time to clearly define what you want to achieve. Write down your goals and get detailed about what success looks like for you. The clearer you are, the easier it will be for you to attract it.

2. Practice Daily Visualization

Set aside time each day to visualize your goals. See yourself already living your desired life. Focus on the emotions you would feel and immerse yourself in the vision as if it's already real. Visualization is a powerful tool for activating the Law of Attraction.

3. Use Affirmations

Affirmations are positive statements that align your thoughts with your goals. Repeat them daily to reinforce your belief in your ability to achieve your desires. For example:

- "I am attracting abundance into my life every day."
- "I am financially free and living my dream life."
- "Opportunities flow to me effortlessly."

4. Feel the Emotions of Your Success

When you visualize or affirm your goals, focus

on the **feeling** of already having achieved them. The stronger the emotion, the more powerful the manifestation process becomes. Feel the joy, excitement, and gratitude of already living your dream life.

5. Trust the Process and Take Inspired Action

Trust that the universe is working in your favor and that opportunities will appear at the right time. But remember, you must also take action. The Law of Attraction works best when you align your thoughts with inspired, purposeful action. When opportunities present themselves, seize them.

6. Practice Gratitude

Gratitude is one of the highest vibrational frequencies you can emit. By being grateful for what you already have, you attract more things to be grateful for. Make gratitude a part of your daily routine, even for small things.

Story: How the Law of Attraction Changed Michael's Life

Michael had always been unhappy with his job. He felt stuck, and although he earned a decent income, he longed for more freedom, more impact, and more financial success.

One day, Michael came across a book on the Law of Attraction and decided to give it a try. He wrote down his desire: "I want to start a successful online business and earn $100,000 per year in passive income."

He created a vision board with images of a laptop, travel destinations, and people working remotely. He visualized himself living this life every morning, feeling the joy and excitement of having financial freedom.

A few months later, Michael got the idea for an online course. He took inspired action, created the course, and launched it. By the end of the year, his income had surpassed $100,000, and he was living the life he had visualized.

Michael's story shows how aligning your thoughts, beliefs, and actions with your desires can unlock the power of the Law of Attraction.

Action Steps to Harness the Law of Attraction

1. **Clarify Your Goals**: Write down your desires in clear and specific terms.
2. **Create a Vision**: Use visualization, affirmations, and a vision board to make your goals real.
3. **Feel the Emotion**: Practice feeling the emotions of already achieving your goals.
4. **Take Inspired Action**: Trust the process and take practical steps toward your goals.
5. **Gratitude**: Cultivate an attitude of gratitude

every day.

Quote to Remember:

"What you think you become. What you feel you attract. What you imagine you create."
- Buddha

Next Up: Chapter 12 -Taking Action and Getting Results

Now that you understand how to use the Law of Attraction, it's time to discuss how to turn your dreams into action. In this chapter, we'll explore how to break your goals down into actionable steps and how to stay motivated through the process.

CHAPTER 12: TAKING ACTION AND GETTING RESULTS

How to Turn Your Dreams into Reality by Taking Consistent Action

---

"The path to success is to take massive, determined action." -Tony Robbins

---

Why Action is the Key to Success

It's easy to get caught up in the excitement of goals and dreams. Visualization, affirmation, and planning are all essential steps in manifesting success but they mean nothing without **action**.

Action is the bridge between where you are now and where you want to be. Without action, you remain in a place of dreaming without doing. The Law of Attraction may help you align your thoughts with your desires, but it's your **effort**,

determination, and **persistence** that will truly bring your dreams to life. It's not enough to simply want something. You have to **act as if** it's already happening and take consistent, purposeful steps toward your goals. Every little action counts, and every step forward gets you closer to your vision.

The Power of Consistency

Success is rarely achieved overnight. The most successful people know that it's not about making a huge leap all at once, but about taking **small, consistent steps** that lead to big results over time. Consistency is the secret ingredient that separates dreamers from achievers.

Here's why consistency is so important:

1. **Building Momentum**: The more you act, the more momentum you build. Even small efforts add up and propel you forward.
2. **Overcoming Obstacles**: Life will throw challenges your way, but consistent action helps you push through setbacks and keep moving toward your goal.

3. **Reinforcing Your Belief**: As you see the results of your efforts, your belief in your ability to achieve your goals will grow.

Breaking Down Your Goals into Actionable Steps

One of the main reasons people fail to achieve

their goals is that they don't break them down into smaller, manageable tasks. It's easy to feel overwhelmed when looking at a big goal, but when you break it down into bite-sized pieces, the process becomes more manageable and less intimidating.

Here's how to break your goals into actionable steps:

1. Define the Goal Clearly

Get specific about what you want to achieve. Instead of saying, "I want to be successful," say, "I want to create a profitable online business earning $100,000 per year within 12 months."

2. Set Milestones

Milestones are the major checkpoints along the way to your goal. For example, for the online business goal, your milestones might include:

- **Month 1**: Market research and niche selection
- **Month 3**: Product development or course creation
- **Month 6**: Website and platform launch
- **Month 9**: First $10,000 in revenue
- **Month 12**: $100,000 in annual revenue

3. Break Milestones into Weekly Tasks

Once you have your milestones, break them down further into **weekly tasks**. For example, if your milestone is to launch your website in 3 months, your weekly tasks might include:

- Week 1: Choose a domain name and hosting provider
- Week 2: Design the website layout
- Week 3: Write content for the website
- Week 4: Launch the website

4. Take Daily Actions

Daily action is where the magic happens. Even on days when you feel uninspired or unmotivated, commit to taking one small action toward your goal. Whether it's researching, writing, or planning, every small step brings you closer to success.

Overcoming Procrastination and Getting Started

Procrastination is one of the biggest obstacles to taking action. It's easy to put off doing the hard work, but procrastination keeps you stuck and frustrated. The key to overcoming procrastination is to get started no matter how small the first step is.

Here's how to overcome procrastination:

1. Break the Task into Small Pieces

The idea of tackling a huge goal can feel overwhelming, so break it down into smaller, more manageable steps. Starting with a small task can make the entire process seem less intimidating.

2. Set a Timer

Commit to working for just **20 minutes** without distractions. Often, once you get started, it's easier to keep going. Use a timer or a productivity technique like the Pomodoro Technique to stay focused.

3. Create a Routine

Having a routine makes it easier to take consistent action. By scheduling regular time blocks to work on your goals, you reduce the mental resistance that comes with trying to fit work into an already busy day.

4. Eliminate Distractions

Turn off notifications, put away your phone, and create a dedicated space to work. The fewer distractions you have, the easier it will be to stay focused and take consistent action.

The Importance of Accountability

Accountability is a powerful motivator. When you share your goals with someone else or set up systems to track your progress, you are more likely to take consistent action and stay committed to your goals.

Here are some ways to hold yourself accountable:

- **Share your goals** with a friend, mentor, or coach who can check in on your progress.
- **Set deadlines** for each step and hold yourself

to them.

- **Use an accountability app** or journal to track your progress daily.

Having someone or something to answer to creates a sense of urgency and keeps you on track. It also provides support and encouragement, which can be vital when facing challenges.

Staying Motivated When the Going Gets Tough

Even the most committed individuals experience moments of doubt and discouragement. But success is rarely a smooth ride. The key to staying motivated is to **keep going**, even when things aren't going as planned.

Here's how to stay motivated:

- **Remember Your "Why"**: Revisit your reasons for pursuing your goal. Whether it's financial freedom, personal growth, or a desire to help others, reconnecting with your purpose will reignite your passion.
- **Celebrate Small Wins**: Acknowledge your progress, even if it's minor. Celebrating small victories will help you stay motivated and reinforce the belief that you are capable of achieving big things.
- **Visualize Your Success**: Remind yourself of the rewards and benefits that will come when you reach your goal. Visualization helps you stay connected to the end result, even when

the journey feels tough.

- **Surround Yourself with Positivity**: Stay inspired by surrounding yourself with people, books, podcasts, and content that uplift and motivate you.

Story: The Power of Consistent Action

When Jessica decided to become a freelance graphic designer, she had no experience in the industry and no portfolio. But she was determined to succeed. She set clear goals, including landing her first client within two months and earning $5,000 per month by the end of the year.

Jessica broke her goal into smaller, manageable steps:

- Week 1: Create a portfolio website
- Week 2: Reach out to potential clients on social media
- Week 3: Offer free work to build testimonials

Every day, Jessica took small, consistent actions toward her goal. Even when things weren't moving as quickly as she hoped, she continued to show up and work. By the end of the year, Jessica had exceeded her $5,000 per month target and had a steady stream of clients. Her success didn't come from one giant leap but from consistent, daily actions that built upon each other over time.

Action Steps for Taking Massive Action

1. **Break Down Your Goal**: Make your goal specific and break it down into smaller, manageable steps.
2. **Set Daily and Weekly Tasks**: Plan daily and weekly actions that will move you closer to your milestone.
3. **Overcome Procrastination**: Commit to taking one small action every day, even when it feels difficult.
4. **Track Your Progress**: Use a journal or app to hold yourself accountable and track your progress regularly.
5. **Stay Motivated**: Celebrate small wins and stay connected to your "why."

Quote to Remember:

"Success is the sum of small efforts, repeated day in and day out." — Robert Collier

---

Next Up: Chapter 13 -Results-Oriented Mindset

Now that we've learned how to take consistent action, it's time to develop a mindset that's focused on getting results. In this chapter, we'll discuss how to think like a results-driven person and maintain your momentum.

CHAPTER 13: RESULTS-ORIENTED MINDSET

How to Cultivate a Results-Driven Mindset for Success

"The greatest mistake you can make in life is to be continually fearing you will make one." - Elbert Hubbard

---

What is a Results-Oriented Mindset?

A **results-oriented mindset** is a mental framework that emphasizes **outcomes over processes**. It's a way of thinking where you focus on what you want to achieve, and you consistently direct your energy and effort toward achieving specific goals and measurable results.

People with a results-oriented mindset prioritize actions that move them closer to their objectives and are motivated by the desire to produce tangible results. They are driven by outcomes and take steps to achieve their goals without getting distracted by minor setbacks or roadblocks.

In contrast, people without a results-oriented mindset may focus more on the tasks themselves or get caught up in perfectionism, leading to delays and inaction.

A results-oriented mindset is crucial because it shifts your focus from mere activity to meaningful progress. It transforms your goal-setting approach, making you more intentional and purpose-driven.

The Characteristics of a Results-Oriented Person

What separates high achievers from those who simply go through the motions is their mindset. Results-oriented individuals share several key characteristics:

1. Clarity of Purpose

A results-oriented person has a crystal-clear vision of what they want to achieve. They set specific, measurable goals and always keep their ultimate objectives in mind. This clarity helps them stay on track and avoid distractions.

2. Focus on Results, Not Just Effort

While effort is important, results-oriented individuals know that effort alone does not guarantee success. They are focused on outcomes and constantly ask themselves, "What actions can I take today to move closer to my goal?"

3. Adaptability

Life rarely goes as planned. A results-oriented person is flexible and willing to adjust their approach when things aren't working. Instead of quitting or giving up, they adapt their strategy until they find a solution that works.

4. Accountability

Results-oriented individuals take full responsibility for their actions. They hold themselves accountable for their progress and are honest about their successes and failures. They track their results and make adjustments when needed.

5. Persistence and Resilience

When challenges arise, a results-oriented person doesn't give up. Instead, they persevere through difficulties and remain focused on their end goal. They view failures as learning opportunities, not roadblocks.

How to Cultivate a Results-Oriented Mindset

Now that we've explored the traits of a results-oriented person, let's dive into how you can develop this mindset for yourself:

1. Set Clear, Measurable Goals

A results-oriented mindset begins with clear, specific, and measurable goals. Vague or ambiguous goals lead to confusion and a lack of direction. To create results, you need to know exactly what you're working toward.

Instead of saying, "I want to be successful," define success in clear terms, such as:

- "I want to increase my passive income by $50,000 by the end of the year."
- "I want to lose 20 pounds in the next 6 months."
- "I want to grow my online business to $10,000 per month in the next 12 months."

Having a specific target gives you something concrete to aim for and allows you to measure your progress along the way.

2. Develop a Focused Action Plan

Once your goals are set, it's time to create a **strategic action plan**. A results-oriented person doesn't just know what they want; they also know how to get there. Break your goals down into smaller, actionable steps, and create a clear plan for achieving each milestone.

For example, if your goal is to increase your passive income by $50,000, your action plan might include:

- **Month 1-3**: Research and identify potential passive income streams (e.g., real estate, affiliate marketing, online courses).
- **Month 4-6**: Launch the chosen passive income project and begin generating revenue.
- **Month 7-9**: Optimize your strategies and focus on scaling your efforts.
- **Month 10-12**: Analyze results and fine-tune your systems to increase revenue.

3. Measure Your Progress Regularly

Results-oriented individuals track their progress to ensure they are on course to achieve their goals. Set regular check-ins (e.g., weekly, monthly) to evaluate your progress. Review your action plan and make necessary adjustments.

Ask yourself:

- What actions have I taken so far?
- How much closer am I to my goal?
- What changes can I make to speed up my progress?

By tracking your progress, you create a sense of accountability and ensure that you are moving toward your desired results.

4. Stay Focused on Solutions

A key trait of results-oriented people is their focus on solutions, not problems. When challenges arise, they don't waste time complaining or dwelling on obstacles. Instead, they focus on finding ways to overcome those challenges.

When facing a setback, ask yourself:

- What can I learn from this?
- What's the best next step to take?
- Who can I reach out to for advice or support?

This mindset helps you maintain momentum and keeps you moving forward even in the face of adversity.

5. Take Massive Action

The most successful people don't just sit back and wait for results to happen, they take **massive action**. A results-oriented mindset means being willing to take bold steps and push yourself outside of your comfort zone.

Remember, success doesn't come from thinking about action, it comes from doing it. The more you act, the more results you will generate. Commit to taking daily, focused action toward your goals, even when it feels uncomfortable.

Overcoming Common Mindset Blocks

Even with a results-oriented mindset, you may encounter some common mental blocks. These blocks can hinder your progress if you don't address them. Let's take a look at a few mindset traps and how to overcome them:

1. Perfectionism

Waiting for the "perfect moment" or "perfect conditions" often leads to inaction. You don't need to be perfect, you just need to take action. Focus on progress, not perfection.

2. Fear of Failure

Fear of failure can paralyze you and prevent you from taking risks.
Remember, failure is part of the journey and an opportunity to learn. Embrace failure as a stepping stone toward success.

3. Self-Doubt

Self-doubt can make you question your ability to achieve your goals. Counter this by focusing on your strengths and past successes. Build confidence through small wins, and remind yourself that you are capable.

4. Lack of Patience

Results take time. It's easy to become frustrated when you don't see immediate results, but success is often a slow process. Stay patient, stay consistent, and trust the process.

Story: Emma's Shift to a Results-Oriented Mindset

Emma had always dreamed of owning her own business, but for years, she let fear and self-doubt hold her back. She was scared of failure and unsure of where to start. But one day, she decided to take a leap of faith and finally launch her business.

She set clear goals: earn $5,000 in her first 6 months, grow her social media presence, and build a customer base. Emma developed an action plan, focused on taking daily steps, and tracked her progress.

Despite facing challenges, Emma remained focused on solutions. She adjusted her approach when things didn't work, learned from failures, and celebrated small wins. Within 6 months, she not only reached her $5,000 goal but also exceeded it. By focusing on results and staying consistent, Emma built the foundation for a successful business.

Action Steps for Developing a Results-Oriented Mindset

1. **Set Clear, Specific Goals**: Define what success looks like for you in clear terms.
2. **Create an Action Plan**: Break your goals down into manageable steps and create a plan for achieving them.
3. **Track Your Progress**: Regularly measure your progress and adjust your approach if necessary.
4. **Focus on Solutions**: When challenges arise, focus on finding solutions instead of dwelling on problems.
5. **Take Action**: Commit to taking daily,

consistent actions toward your goals.

Quote to Remember:

"Success is the sum of small efforts, repeated day in and day out." — Robert Collier

---

Next Up: Chapter 14 — Building Habits for Success

Now that we've developed a results-oriented mindset, it's time to discuss how to build the habits that will support your success. In this chapter, we'll explore the habits of highly successful people and how you can incorporate them into your daily life.

CHAPTER 10: THE VISION BOARD

How to Use Visualization to Manifest Your Dreams and Goals

"A goal without a plan is just a wish."
-Antoine de Saint-Exupéry

What is a Vision Board?

A vision board is a physical or digital collection of images, words, and quotes that represent your **goals**, **dreams**, and **desires**. It's essentially a visual representation of what you want to manifest in your life.

Creating a vision board allows you to get clear on your aspirations and brings them into focus. By visualizing your dreams daily, you begin to reprogram your brain to recognize opportunities that align with your goals. It's a powerful tool for manifesting your ideal life, not just because it's fun to create, but because it helps you **feel** and **experience** your goals in the present moment.

The Power of Visualization

Visualization is the process of imagining your goals as already achieved. It's the ability to see yourself succeeding in your mind, which sends powerful messages to your subconscious. Visualization is a practice used by many successful people, including athletes, entrepreneurs, and top performers.

Studies show that the brain doesn't differentiate between **real experiences** and **imagined experiences**. This means when you visualize your goals and achievements, your brain treats them almost as if they are already happening. This mental rehearsal helps you develop the necessary skills, mindset, and motivation to make your vision a reality.

How to Create a Vision Board That Works

Creating a vision board is more than just cutting out pretty pictures. It's about aligning your **goals**, **values**, and **purpose** with the images you place on the board. Here's how to create one that works:

1. Clarify Your Goals

Before you start cutting out images, take time to clarify what you want to achieve. Ask yourself:

- What does my ideal life look like?
- What are my financial, health, career, and

relationship goals?

- What does success mean to me?

The clearer you are about your goals, the more effective your vision board will be in helping you manifest them.

2. Gather Your Materials

To create a physical vision board, you will need:

- A board or large poster (or you can use a digital tool like Canva or Pinterest)
- Magazines, printouts, or online images that resonate with your goals
- Scissors, glue, or tape (for a physical board)

For a digital vision board, you can use tools like Canva, Pinterest, or even a simple PowerPoint presentation.

3. Choose Meaningful Images and Words

Select images that speak to you emotionally. Your vision board should feel inspiring and energizing. Look for:

- **Pictures** that represent the lifestyle you want, such as travel, health, career success, family, etc.
- **Words or affirmations** that empower you and align with your values. Phrases like "financial freedom," "health and vitality," or "unstoppable" are good examples.
- **Symbols** that represent abundance, success,

or specific goals you want to achieve.

4. Arrange Your Vision Board

Arrange the images and words on your board in a way that feels right to you. There's no "wrong" way to arrange it, but make sure the most important goals stand out. As you do this, focus on how it feels. The more you connect with the **emotion** of your dreams, the stronger the board will be in bringing those dreams into reality.

5. Place It Somewhere Visible

Once your vision board is complete, place it somewhere where you'll see it every day — on your bedroom wall, your office, or as your desktop wallpaper. The more frequently you look at it, the more you reinforce your goals and remind yourself of your purpose.

How to Use Your Vision Board

Your vision board is a tool for **daily visualization** and motivation. Here's how to use it effectively:

1. Visualize Daily

Spend 5-10 minutes each day in front of your vision board, focusing on the images and feeling the emotions of already having what you desire. Imagine living that life — visualize the details, such as the sights, sounds, and feelings. Make it as real as possible in your mind.

2. Affirmations and Gratitude

Along with visualization, practice affirmations and gratitude. Say affirmations like:

- "I am financially free and abundant."
- "I am a healthy, successful, and confident person."
- "Every day, I am closer to my goals."

Also, feel gratitude for what you already have and for the future success you are calling in. Gratitude is one of the most powerful energy sources to manifest your desires.

3. Take Inspired Action

While your vision board is a powerful tool for manifestation, it's important to remember that **action is key**. Each time you look at your vision board, ask yourself:

- What actions can I take today to move closer to my goal?
- How can I align my behavior with my vision?

Your vision board will serve as a constant reminder to take consistent, inspired action toward your dreams.

Story: The Vision Board That Changed Everything

Sarah had always dreamed of starting her own business. She wanted financial freedom, a healthy work-life balance, and the ability to travel. But for years, she felt stuck in her 9-to-5 job, unsure of how to make her dreams a reality.

One day, she attended a workshop on manifestation and was introduced to the concept of vision boards. Inspired, she went home, clarified her goals, and created a powerful vision board with images of business success, travel destinations, and a vibrant lifestyle.

Sarah placed her vision board on her office wall, and every day, she visualized herself living the life she desired. She felt the excitement of running a business, traveling to exotic locations, and experiencing freedom.

Over the next few months, Sarah began to take small steps toward her goal:

- She started researching her business idea.
- She created a plan and set clear milestones.
- She invested in herself by taking courses and networking with others in the entrepreneurial community.

Within a year, Sarah had launched her online business. It was a struggle at first, but she remained focused on her vision and took consistent action. Today, Sarah runs a thriving business and travels the world, living the life she once only dreamed of — all thanks to her vision board.

Action Steps to Create Your Vision Board

1. **Clarify Your Goals**: Take time to define your dreams and aspirations clearly.
2. **Gather Materials**: Collect images, words, and symbols that represent your goals.
3. **Create Your Vision Board**: Arrange the images on a physical or digital board in a way that inspires you.
4. **Visualize Daily**: Spend time each day in front of your board, feeling the emotions of already living your goals.
5. **Take Action**: Use your vision board as motivation to take daily inspired actions toward your dreams.

Quote to Remember:

"Your vision will become clear only when you can look into your own heart.
Who looks outside, dreams; who looks inside, awakens." -Carl Jung

---

Next Up: Chapter 11 — The Law of Attraction

Now that you've learned how to visualize and manifest your dreams, it's time to dive deeper into the **Law of Attraction** and understand how to attract the opportunities, people, and circumstances that will bring your vision to life.

CHAPTER 14: BUILDING HABITS FOR SUCCESS

How to Cultivate the Habits of Highly Effective People

"We are what we repeatedly do. Excellence, then, is not an act, but a habit." - Aristotle

---

Why Habits Are Crucial for Success

Success isn't about one monumental act; it's about the **small, everyday actions** you take. Habits are the foundation upon which success is built. They are the behaviors, routines, and patterns that you do automatically, without thinking. Whether you realize it or not, your habits dictate the quality of your life and your potential for success.

To become successful, you must build habits that support your goals. The most successful people didn't get where they are by accident. They developed specific habits that helped them stay productive, focused, and motivated. The beauty of habits is that once they're ingrained, they require little mental effort to maintain, but they yield significant long-term results.

If you want to unlock your potential and consistently achieve great results, you need to develop the right habits.

The Power of Small Habits

Small habits may seem insignificant at first, but over time, they compound to create significant change. This is known as the **Compound Effect**. Just like saving small amounts of money each day leads to long-term wealth, small habits practiced consistently lead to massive success.

For example, consider the habit of reading 10 pages of a book every day. At first, it seems trivial, but over the course of a year, that's over 3,600 pages — the equivalent of reading several books. This consistent action can lead to greater knowledge, personal growth, and opportunities.

Small habits, when done consistently, can produce extraordinary results over time. The key is **consistency**.

The Key Habits of Highly Successful People

Successful people don't just work hard; they work **smart**. They have developed a set of habits that help them stay productive, focused, and aligned with their goals. Here are some of the most common habits of highly effective people:

1. Morning Routines

Many successful people swear by their morning routines. A productive morning sets the tone for the rest of the day. The key is to start your day with intention and purpose. Here are some habits to include in your morning routine:

- **Wake up early**: Many successful people wake up before 5 a.m. to get a jump start on their day.
- **Exercise**: Physical activity helps boost energy levels and mental clarity.
- **Mindfulness**: Meditation, journaling, or simply reflecting on your goals helps center your mind.
- **Read or listen to podcasts**: Reading or consuming educational content helps you learn something new every day.

2. Goal Setting

Highly successful people are always focused on their goals. They know exactly what they want to achieve and how to get there. They break down their larger goals into smaller, actionable steps and track their progress regularly. Setting goals allows them to stay focused and motivated.

3. Time Management

Effective time management is a habit that

separates high achievers from those who struggle. Successful people prioritize their time by focusing on what's important and eliminating distractions. They use strategies like:

- **Time blocking**: Allocating specific blocks of time to specific tasks.
- **The Pomodoro Technique**: Working in focused intervals with short breaks.
- **The 80/20 Rule (Pareto Principle)**: Focusing on the 20% of tasks that will yield 80% of the results.

4. Continuous Learning

The most successful people understand that learning doesn't stop once they finish school or hit a milestone. They commit to continuous self-improvement and are always seeking new knowledge. They read books, attend seminars, listen to podcasts, and seek mentorship to expand their knowledge and skills.

5. Networking and Building Relationships

Success is rarely achieved in isolation. Building a strong network of supportive, like-minded people is a common habit among successful individuals. They make it a priority to nurture relationships, collaborate with others, and seek opportunities for growth through their network.

6. Exercise and Physical Health

The mind and body are interconnected. If you're not taking care of your body, it's harder to stay focused, energized, and motivated. Successful people make exercise and physical health a priority. Regular physical activity helps to improve mental clarity, reduce stress, and increase energy levels.

How to Build Powerful Habits

Building effective habits doesn't happen overnight. It requires patience, discipline, and consistency. Here's how to build habits that will support your success:

1. Start Small and Be Consistent

When starting a new habit, don't try to change everything at once. Start with small, manageable changes and be consistent. If you try to overhaul your entire life all at once, you're likely to get overwhelmed and quit. Focus on one habit at a time and build on it gradually.

For example, if you want to start exercising, don't aim for an hour a day right away. Start with 10-15 minutes a day, then gradually increase the duration as the habit becomes ingrained.

2. Create a Trigger for Your Habit

Habits are easier to form when you associate them with an existing behavior. This is called "habit stacking." For example, if you already drink coffee every morning, use that time as a trigger to practice gratitude or read a few pages of a book. By stacking a new habit onto an existing one, you make it easier to remember and implement.

3. Track Your Progress

Tracking your progress is essential for maintaining motivation and consistency. Use a habit tracker or journal to monitor your daily efforts. Celebrate your progress and make adjustments if needed. Small wins along the way keep you motivated and reinforce your commitment to the habit.

4. Remove Temptations and Distractions

Environment plays a significant role in habit formation. Remove distractions and temptations that might undermine your new habits. If you're trying to read more, place a book on your desk where you can easily see it. If you're working on losing weight, avoid keeping junk food in the house. By controlling your environment, you make it easier to stick to your new habits.

5. Be Patient and Stay Persistent

Building new habits takes time. Research suggests that it takes an average of **66 days** to form a new habit, but it can vary. The key is to be patient and persistent. Don't expect immediate results. Just keep showing up and doing the work. Over time, your habits will become second nature.

How to Break Bad Habits

Bad habits can hold you back and prevent you from reaching your full potential. But breaking bad habits is possible with the right approach. Here's how to do it:

1. Identify the Trigger

Bad habits are often triggered by certain cues, such as stress, boredom, or even specific locations. By identifying the trigger, you can either remove the cue or replace the bad habit with a healthier one.

2. Replace the Habit

Instead of focusing on eliminating the bad habit, replace it with a positive habit. For example, if you tend to snack on unhealthy food when you're bored, replace the habit with going for a walk or drinking a glass of water.

3. Use Accountability

Share your goal to break the bad habit with a friend or mentor who can hold you accountable. Accountability makes it more likely that you'll stay committed to breaking the habit.

4. Forgive Yourself

Don't beat yourself up if you slip up. Breaking habits is a process, and setbacks are part of the journey. Be kind to yourself, forgive yourself, and keep moving forward.

James had always struggled with productivity. He'd wake up late, rush through his day, and never felt like he accomplished much. But one day, he decided to transform his mornings.

James started waking up an hour earlier to fit in exercise, reading, and planning his day. He started small, committing to 10 minutes of exercise and 15 minutes of reading each morning. Over time, his energy levels increased, and he felt more focused throughout the day. His newfound morning routine set the tone for the rest of his day, and within months, he noticed a significant improvement in his productivity and overall wellbeing.

Action Steps for Building Habits for Success

1. **Start Small**: Begin with one new habit at a time and focus on consistency.
2. **Create a Trigger**: Stack your new habit on top of an existing behavior.
3. **Track Progress**: Use a habit tracker or journal to monitor your efforts.
4. **Remove Temptations**: Adjust your environment to support your new habit.
5. **Be Patient**: Understand that building a habit takes time. Stay persistent.
6. **Replace Bad Habits**: Identify triggers for bad habits and replace them with healthier alternatives.

Quote to Remember:

"Your habits will determine your future."
-Jack Canfield

Next Up: Chapter 15 — Building Your Dream Team

Now that we've covered building habits, it's time to discuss the power of collaboration and how to build a strong network and team that supports your success.

CHAPTER 15: BUILDING YOUR DREAM TEAM

How to Assemble a Team That Will Help You Achieve Your Goals

"If you want to go fast, go alone. If you want to go far, go together." -African Proverb

---

The Power of Teamwork

No one achieves great success alone. Even the most successful billionaires, entrepreneurs, and high achievers have a strong team behind them. Building a dream team is not just about hiring the right people, it's about creating a collaborative environment that fosters growth, creativity, and mutual success.

The concept of a **dream team** is not just for sports teams or big corporations; it applies to anyone looking to scale their business or personal endeavors. Whether you're growing a small business, building passive income streams, or pursuing a personal project, surrounding yourself with the right people can dramatically improve your chances of success.

A dream team is composed of individuals with complementary skills, diverse perspectives, and a shared commitment to a common goal. When you collaborate with others, you can leverage their strengths, ideas, and resources to accelerate your journey toward success.

Why You Need a Dream Team

There are several reasons why building a strong team is essential for achieving financial, time, and mental freedom:

1. Leverage Expertise

You can't do everything on your own. Even if you're highly skilled in one area, there are many other aspects of business and life that require expertise. By building a team of experts, you can delegate tasks to people who are more qualified and experienced in specific areas.

2. Accelerated Growth

A great team can help you grow faster. With the right people in place, you can scale your efforts, reach more people, and take on more projects without burning yourself out. A team allows you to focus on the big picture while others take care of the details.

3. Increased Creativity and Innovation

When you bring together diverse minds with different backgrounds and experiences, you create an environment where new ideas and solutions can emerge. Collaboration often sparks creativity and innovation that you might not have come up with on your own.

4. Shared Responsibility

A strong team allows you to share the weight of responsibility. You don't have to carry all the burdens alone. When you delegate tasks, you free yourself from the pressure of doing everything and give your team the opportunity to contribute to the overall success.

5. Accountability

Having a team creates accountability. Each person on the team is responsible for a specific part of the process, which helps keep everyone on track. When you work alone, it's easy to procrastinate or let things slide. A team ensures that everyone is working toward a common goal and meeting deadlines.

Key Roles in a Dream Team

A successful dream team consists of various key

roles that complement one another. These roles vary depending on your goals and business type, but here are some of the most important ones to consider:

1. The Visionary

The visionary is the person who sets the big picture and direction for the team. This is often the founder or leader who creates the vision, mission, and overall strategy. The visionary is responsible for staying focused on long-term goals and motivating the team to work toward them.

2. The Operator

The operator is responsible for executing the plans and strategies put in place by the visionary. This person manages the day-to-day operations, ensures that tasks are being completed, and solves any operational challenges that arise. The operator ensures that the team is moving in the right direction and that deadlines are met.

3. The Specialist

Every team needs specialists who can bring in-depth knowledge and expertise in specific areas. These can include roles like:

- **Marketing experts** who help with branding, advertising, and customer acquisition.
- **Financial advisors** who manage budgeting, accounting, and investments.

- **Legal professionals** who handle contracts, compliance, and intellectual property.
- **Product developers** who create and improve products or services.

4. The Communicator

Effective communication is essential for a successful team. The communicator is the person who ensures that information flows smoothly among all team members. They act as the liaison, keeping everyone updated and ensuring that all team members are aligned with the goals and strategies.

5. The Supporter

The supporter is the person who ensures the team's morale remains high. They handle the emotional and psychological aspects of the team's dynamics, helping to resolve conflicts, motivate team members, and keep everyone feeling supported. The supporter is key in maintaining a positive and collaborative environment.

How to Build Your Dream Team

Building your dream team doesn't happen overnight, and it's not as simple as hiring people and assigning them roles. Here are some important steps to help you build a team that will support your vision and help you reach your goals.

1. Identify Your Needs

Before you can build a dream team, you need to identify what roles you need to fill. Think about the specific skills and expertise that you require in order to achieve your goals. What are your strengths, and where do you need help? Understanding your needs will allow you to recruit the right people for the job.

2. Hire for Attitude, Not Just Skills

While skills are important, attitude is just as crucial. You want people who are passionate, motivated, and committed to your vision. Look for individuals who are aligned with your values, work ethic, and long-term goals. Skills can be taught, but a positive attitude and a strong work ethic are much harder to instill.

3. Create a Collaborative Culture

Building a dream team requires creating a culture of collaboration. Encourage open communication, respect for diverse opinions, and a shared commitment to the team's success. Foster a supportive environment where team members feel safe to share their ideas and challenges.

4. Provide Growth Opportunities

Your team members will be more engaged and motivated if they see opportunities for personal and professional growth. Provide regular feedback, encourage skill development, and offer opportunities for advancement within the team. A dream team is one that continues to evolve and improve over time.

5. Delegate Effectively

Once you have the right team in place, it's important to delegate effectively. Trust your team members to do their jobs and resist the temptation to micromanage. Effective delegation allows you to focus on your strengths and ensures that everyone is contributing to the team's success.

The Importance of a Supportive Network

In addition to your core team, you should also consider building a broader network of mentors, advisors, and collaborators. A strong support network can offer guidance, open doors, and provide opportunities that will help you accelerate your growth.

Here's how to build your network:

- **Seek Mentorship**: Find people who have already achieved what you want to achieve and learn from them.
- **Attend Industry Events**: Networking events, conferences, and seminars are great opportunities to meet people who can help you on your journey.
- **Collaborate with Others**: Look for opportunities to collaborate with others in your industry. Joint ventures can help you

reach a wider audience and create new revenue streams.

Story: Sarah's Journey to Building Her Dream Team

Sarah had always dreamed of building a successful online business. At first, she tried to do everything on her own, from marketing to customer service. But after months of struggling, she realized she couldn't do it all. She needed help.

Sarah began to build her dream team by first identifying the roles she needed to fill. She hired a marketing specialist, a customer service manager, and an accountant. Each person brought unique skills and expertise, and together, they were able to take Sarah's business to the next level.

Sarah trusted her team, delegated effectively, and encouraged a collaborative culture. As a result, the business grew exponentially, and Sarah was able to step back from the day-to-day operations and focus on scaling her business even further.

Action Steps for Building Your Dream Team

1. **Identify the key roles you need** to help you reach your goals.
2. **Hire for attitude, not just skills** — seek people who align with your values and vision.
3. **Create a collaborative culture** where open communication and respect are prioritized.

4. **Delegate effectively** — trust your team and allow them to contribute to their fullest potential.
5. **Build a strong support network** of mentors, advisors, and collaborators.

Quote to Remember:

"Alone we can do so little; together we can do so much." -Helen Keller

---

Next Up: Chapter 16 — Conclusion: Your Path to Financial, Time, and Mental Freedom

Now that you've built your dream team, it's time to wrap up your journey to financial, time, and mental freedom. In the final chapter, we'll bring everything together and outline the steps you need to continue on your path to success.

CHAPTER 16: CONCLUSION

Your Path to Financial, Time, and Mental Freedom

"The future belongs to those who believe in the beauty of their dreams." — Eleanor Roosevelt

---

Chapter 16: Conclusion

You've Made It to the Finish Line

Congratulations! You've completed the journey through **The Billionaire's Guide**, and now you have all the tools you need to take control of your financial, time, and mental freedom. Throughout this book, we've discussed how to achieve success, from mastering the law of attraction to building habits that support your vision, from understanding the principles of passive income to assembling your dream team.

The path you've been on is a road less traveled by most people, but it is the road that leads to **true freedom**, the kind of freedom that gives you control over your time, the ability to earn without working constantly, and the mental peace that comes from knowing you are in charge of your destiny.

The Key Takeaways:

As you embark on the next chapter of your life, let's review some of the most important lessons and insights from this guide:

1. **Develop the Right Mindset**

   Your mindset is the foundation of everything you do. Believe in yourself, adopt an abundance mentality, and understand that **your thoughts shape your reality**. The law of attraction and the power of positive thinking will guide you to success.

2. **Master Your Time**

   Time is the most valuable resource you have. To achieve true freedom, you must learn to manage your time effectively. Prioritize high-impact tasks, eliminate distractions, and delegate whenever possible. A strong morning routine can set the tone for a productive day, and the Pareto Principle (80/20 rule) can help you focus on the 20% of activities that yield 80% of the results.

3. **Create Multiple Streams of Passive Income**
   Wealth is built through **leverage**. The more streams of income you have, the more freedom you create for yourself. From investments to digital products, business ventures to side hustles, diversifying your income will give you the financial cushion you need for freedom.
4. **Build Good Habits**
   Your habits are the building blocks of success. Small, consistent actions compounded over time lead to extraordinary results. Whether it's reading daily, exercising regularly, or setting clear goals, your habits define the person you become. Make them work for you, not against you.
5. **Assemble Your Dream Team**
   Success is not a solo journey. Surround yourself with people who complement your strengths, support your vision, and help you scale your efforts. Whether it's business partners, employees, mentors, or advisors, your team will be the force that propels you toward your goals.
6. **Financial Management is Key**
   Understanding how to manage and grow your wealth is crucial for maintaining long-term freedom. Learn the principles of cash flow management, and never stop improving your financial literacy. A clear, actionable plan will help you preserve and grow your wealth.

Taking Action: The Next Steps

Knowledge is only powerful when it's put into action. It's time for you to take everything you've learned and start applying it. The road to freedom is not without challenges, but it is definitely worth it.

Here's how you can start:

1. Create Your Vision and Set Goals

Go back to the drawing board. What does your dream life look like? What goals do you need to achieve in order to get there? Break your goals into smaller, actionable steps and make a detailed plan. Your vision board can serve as a powerful reminder of your dreams.

2. Take the First Step

You don't need to have everything figured out before you take action. Start today. Whether it's setting up a savings account, researching passive income streams, or scheduling time for a new habit, every action brings you closer to your goal.

3. Measure Your Progress

Track your progress regularly. Make sure you're hitting your targets, whether they're financial, personal, or professional. Celebrate your wins, however small, and learn from any setbacks. Success is not linear, it's a series of steps forward, with occasional detours.

4. Stay Committed

Remember that consistency is key. The road to financial, time, and mental freedom is built on **small, consistent actions** over time. Stay committed to your vision, and don't get discouraged by challenges or setbacks. Every successful person has faced obstacles — what matters is how you respond.

5. Expand Your Knowledge

Never stop learning. The world of personal finance, business, and success is constantly evolving. Stay up-to-date on the latest strategies, tools, and technologies that can help you continue to grow. Seek mentorship, attend workshops, read books, and keep improving your skill set.

The Journey Continues

This book is just the beginning. You have all the tools and knowledge to set yourself on the path to success, but it's up to you to take the first step and continue forward. Remember, it's not about the destination, it's about the journey.

You are now equipped with the mindset, strategies, and practical tools to achieve the **freedom** you deserve. Whether you're working on your business, creating passive income, or simply enjoying more time with your loved ones, the possibilities are endless.

Final Thoughts: Your Financial, Time, and Mental

Freedom

The freedom you're seeking isn't just about having money, it's about having the **freedom to live life on your own terms**, to make decisions that align with your values and passions, and to spend your time doing what you truly love. This freedom allows you to live with purpose, intention, and peace of mind.

Remember, financial freedom is within your reach. By leveraging your time, your money, and your skills, you can create the life you've always dreamed of. Now, go out and make it happen.

Quote to Remember:

"Success is the sum of small efforts, repeated day in and day out." — Robert Collier

---

Your journey to financial, time, and mental freedom starts today. Take the first step and embrace the power within you to create the life you deserve. The future is waiting for you!

ABOUT THE AUTHOR

Godfred Akakpo

Godfred Akakpo's journey to success is one of perseverance, growth, and the power of transformation. Raised in humble beginnings, Godfred's father was a dedicated fire officer, and his mother was a resourceful businesswoman. From an early age, he learned the values of hard work, discipline, and resourcefulness. However, it wasn't until he uncovered the transformative secrets of financial independence and personal freedom that his life truly began to change.

Godfred's path wasn't always clear. He worked across multiple sectors and held various roles, gaining invaluable experience that spanned from educational management to community development. He served as a member of the management team at Samess Elite International School in Accra, Ghana, where he helped shape the future of young minds. Additionally, he actively participated in several community-building projects and contributed as a financial committee member at Berakahouse Chapel International, Accra, Ghana.

Throughout these experiences, Godfred encountered challenges common to many people, the limited time, financial constraints, and a lack of systems to leverage his resources. It was these challenges that pushed him to seek out the secrets to financial, time, and mental freedom principles that not only transformed his own life but also the lives of those around him. In writing The Billionaire's Guide, Godfred shares the practical tools and strategies that helped him overcome obstacles and build a life of freedom and success. This book is not just a theory; it is a blueprint born from real world experience, designed to help others break free from the conventional systems that limit them.

Godfred believes that everyone, no matter their background, can achieve financial independence and create the life they desire. Through the lessons in this book, he hopes to empower others to take control of their finances, time, and mindset just as he did.

www.ingramcontent.com/pod-product-compliance
Lightning Source LLC
LaVergne TN
LVHW022227200926
848481LV00006B/2155
9789988528300